Gods of Legend

ATHENA

ERIC BRAUN

BLACK
RABBIT
BOOKS

BOLT

Bolt is published by Black Rabbit Books
P.O. Box 3263, Mankato, Minnesota, 56002.
www.blackrabbitbooks.com
Copyright © 2018 Black Rabbit Books

Marysa Storm, editor; Michael Sellner, designer;
Omay Ayres, photo researcher

Library of Congress Cataloging-in-Publication Data
Names: Braun, Eric, 1971- author.
Title: Athena / by Eric Braun.
Description: Mankato, Minnesota : Black Rabbit Books, [2018] | Series: Bolt.
Gods of legend | Includes bibliographical references and index. | Audience:
Age 9-12. | Audience: Grade 4 to 6.
Identifiers: LCCN 2016049944 (print) | LCCN 2016058509 (ebook) | ISBN
9781680721362 (library binding) | ISBN 9781680722000 (e-book) | ISBN
9781680724455 (paperback)
Subjects: LCSH: Athena (Greek deity)–Juvenile literature. | Mythology,
Greek–Juvenile literature.
Classification: LCC BL820.M6 B73 2018 (print) | LCC BL820.M6 (ebook) |
DDC 398.20938/01–dc23
LC record available at https://lccn.loc.gov/2016049944

Printed in the United States at CG Book Printers,
North Mankato, Minnesota, 56003. 3/17

Image Credits

CONTENTS

CHAPTER 1

An ANCIENT Story

Athena was a powerful goddess. Her father was Zeus, ruler of the Greek gods. He looked to Athena for advice. She was his favorite child. But Athena was far from his favorite in the beginning.

Before Athena was born, Zeus got bad news. He heard that his wife would have a child stronger than he was. But Zeus wanted to stay the strongest. The god turned his wife into a fly and swallowed her.

Athena's Inventions

Greek stories say Athena invented many things.

BRIDLE

FLUTE

SHIP

CHARIOT

Warfare and Wisdom

Inside Zeus, his wife built **armor**. The banging gave Zeus a horrible headache. The pain was like no other. Zeus asked his son to help him. His son grabbed an ax and split open Zeus' head. Out of the god's head stepped Athena.

Athena came out of Zeus fully grown. Stories say she was wearing armor too. She became the goddess of war. She also taught people about arts and crafts. Athena was very wise.

CHAPTER 2

Greek
MYTHOLOGY

The story of Athena is a Greek **myth**. **Ancient** people told stories to explain the world. They believed gods lived among them. They believed the gods made events, such as storms, happen.

Greek myths were written down around 750 BC. But the Greeks had shared the stories for hundreds of years before.

MOUNT OLYMPUS
where the gods lived

ATHENS
city named for Athena

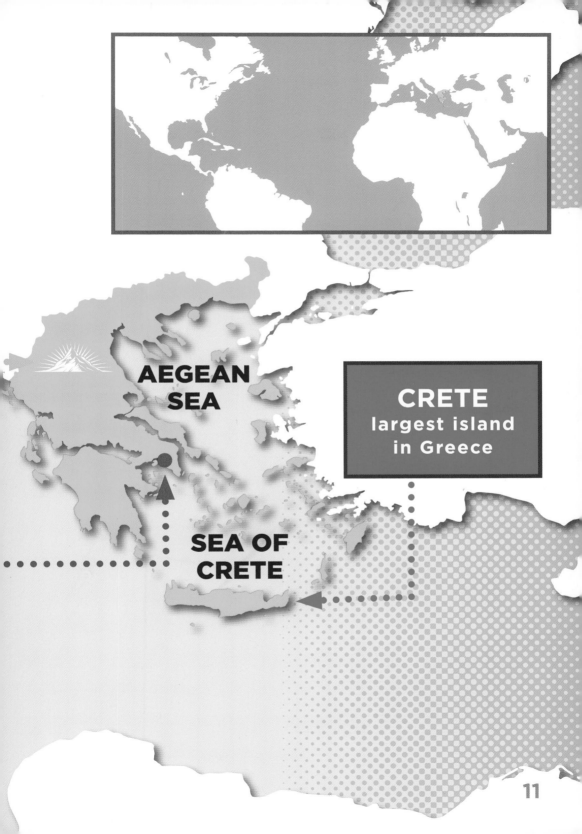

AEGEAN SEA

CRETE
largest island
in Greece

SEA OF
CRETE

Even Temper

Stories say Athena rarely got mad. She stayed calm when bad things happened. Other gods asked her to settle **arguments**.

Athena did lose her temper sometimes. In one story, she lost a weaving contest to a human. Athena became so angry, she turned the woman into a spider.

Appearance and Symbols

Most ancient images show Athena wearing armor and a helmet. She is often seen with an owl. The owl stands for **wisdom** and understanding.

Athena is also pictured with olive trees. Stories say that Athena gave olive trees to ancient Greeks. They used the trees for wood, food, and oil. As thanks, the Greeks named Athens after her.

Athens was the center of Greek art and writing.

HELMET

OWL

ATHENA

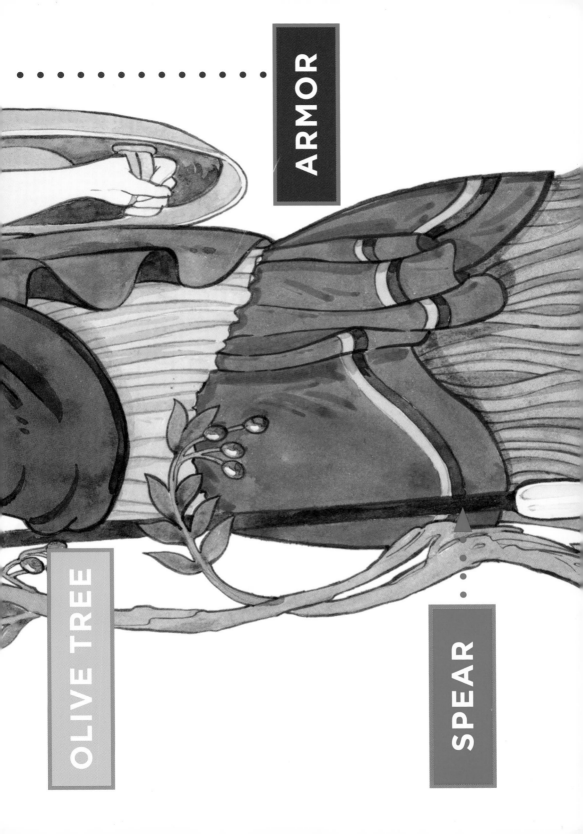

ARMOR

OLIVE TREE

SPEAR

CHAPTER 3

ATHENA and People

In some stories, Athena helped humans. But she would also punish them. The goddess judged their behavior. She decided what they deserved. People believed she was fair. But her punishments could be very cruel.

Stories say Athena helped the hero Hercules several times.

Punishing Soldiers

One story tells how Athena punished many people. Athena had helped the Greeks win a war. But they did not give proper thanks. Athena became angry. She caused some of the soldiers to die on their way home. She made others get lost.

• •

It took one soldier, Odysseus, 10 years to make it home.

THE PARTHENON

People built temples **dedicated** to the gods. Athena's temple was the Parthenon.

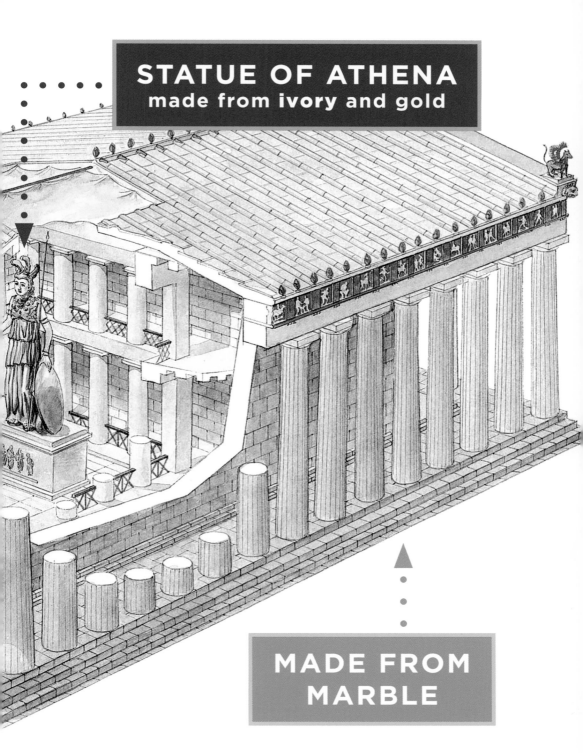

STATUE OF ATHENA
made from **ivory** and gold

MADE FROM MARBLE

CHAPTER 4

Importance of

Athena was one of many Greek goddesses. People today know many of the gods' stories from a poem. It is called *The Iliad*.

In 146 BC, the Romans took over Greece. The Romans liked the Greek myths. They made them their own. They renamed Athena as Minerva. Zeus became the god Jupiter.

25

ATHENA
through Time

1,000 BC

750 BC

The Iliad is written.

People begin building Athena's temple.

447 BC

432 BC

100 BC

146 BC

The temple opens.

Rome takes over Greece.

ancient (AYN-shunt)—from a time long ago

argument (AHR-gyuh-muhnt)—an angry disagreement

armor (AR-muhr)—a protective outer layer

bridle (BRAHYD-l)—a device that fits on a horse's head and that is used for guiding and controlling the horse

dedicated (DED-i-key-tid)—devoted to a cause, ideal, or purpose

ivory (AHY-vuh-ree)—a hard, white substance that forms the tusks of elephants and other animals

myth (MITH)—a story told to explain a practice, belief, or natural occurrence

university (yoo-nuh-VUR-si-tee)—an institution of higher learning that grants degrees

wisdom (WIZ-duhm)—the natural ability to understand things that most other people cannot understand

Athena Today

People no longer believe Greek gods exist. But they still enjoy stories about them. A U.S. military school uses Athena's helmet as a symbol. So do some **universities**. Her story is from a long time ago. But it is still important today.